MW01233724

c/

The ELEANOR ROOSEVELT
You Never Knew

BY JAMES LINCOLN COLLIER

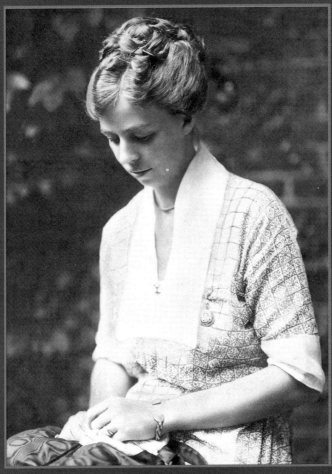

Children's Press®
A Division of Scholastic Inc.
New York Toronto London Auckland Sydney
Mexico City New Delhi Hong Kong
Danbury, Connecticut

Library of Congress Cataloging-in-Publication Data

Collier, James Lincoln, 1928-
  The Eleanor Roosevelt you never knew / James Lincoln Collier ;
[illustrations by Greg Copeland].
       v. cm.
  Includes bibliographical references (p.   ) and index.
  Contents: The ugly duckling — The fateful marriage — Tragedy strikes —
First lady — Life alone.
  ISBN 0-516-24425-6
  1. Roosevelt, Eleanor, 1884-1962—Juvenile literature. 2. Presidents'
spouses—United States—Biography—Juvenile literature. [1. Roosevelt, Eleanor,
1884-1962. 2. First ladies. 3. Women—Biography.] I. Copeland, Greg, ill. II.
Title.
  E807.1.R48C65 2004
  973.917'092—dc22

                              2003028304

Illustrations by Greg Copeland
Book design by A. Natacha Pimentel C.

Photographs © 2004: Corbis Images: 1, 34, 37, 43, 46, 61, 71, 74, 76 bottom
(Bettmann), 48 (Underwood & Underwood), 13, 23, 51, 76 top; Franklin D. Roosevelt
Library Digital Archives: back cover, cover, 4, 9, 11, 15, 17, 20, 25, 26, 28, 29, 30,
31, 40, 55, 57, 64, 67, 68, 73, 76 center.

CONTENTS

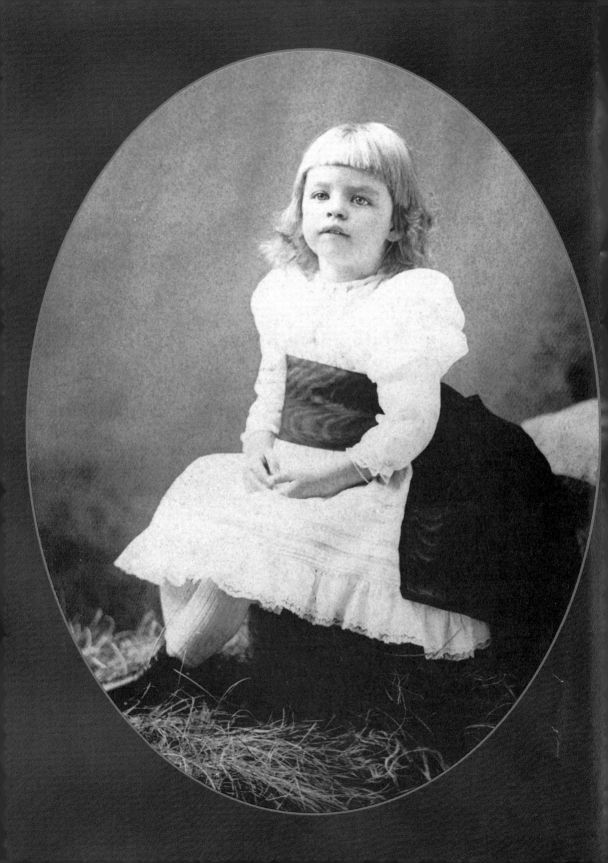

Chapter 1

THE UGLY DUCKLING

S HE WAS A SHY, TIMID LITTLE GIRL who felt that she was never good enough for her parents. She was sure that she was not pretty. She was certainly intelligent, but she did better in school at some subjects than others. She was not good at sports and dancing and didn't learn to swim until she was an adult. And yet, she grew up to be the most famous woman of her day, sometimes called "First Lady of the World."

The children of the wealthy were often photographed in fanciful settings. Here, little Eleanor appears to be sitting on a pile of hay, although the photo was actually taken in a studio.

Today she is remembered as one of America's great heroines, without question the most influential president's wife we have ever had.

In fact, little Eleanor had much to live up to. Her parents were two of the most glamorous members of high society in New York City during the 1880s. Her father, Elliott Roosevelt, was handsome, a great horseback rider who played polo well and also hunted fox and big game. He was friendly and great fun to be with. His brother Theodore would eventually become the much-admired president Teddy Roosevelt, for whom teddy bears were named.

Eleanor's mother was Anna Hall. When Elliott was first getting to know Anna, he wrote a friend that she was "a tall slender fair-haired little beauty—just out [having made her social debut] and a great belle." According to one historian, she was "acclaimed as one of society's most glamorous women." In 1882 Elliott and Anna were married. By 1884 Anna knew she was going to have a baby. She and Elliott wanted a boy. Instead, on October 11, 1884, they had a girl, whom they named Anna Eleanor Roosevelt. Eleanor, thus, was a disappointment to her parents from the start. Making matters worse, she was not a very pretty child. She had beautiful soft blue eyes—all her life people would say so. And she had long blonde hair. But her jaw was a little too small, and her teeth too prominent. No wonder she began to think that she would never be good enough for her handsome and popular parents. This feeling made her shy and fearful—afraid of the dark, of horses, of snakes. She became a lonely child who did not mix easily with other children. She tried desperately to be good, to please her parents. She said, "I was a solemn child, without beauty and painfully shy and I seemed like a little old woman entirely lacking in the spontaneous joy and mirth of youth." Her mother sometimes called her "Granny."

There was, however, another reason Eleanor lacked "joy and mirth." We must understand that in the second half of the nineteenth century, the United States was divided into a very small number of "haves" and a large number of "have-nots." At the bottom of the social ladder was the majority, the laboring people who worked very hard for long hours at low wages. Many of them had been driven off farms by hard times and had come to the cities to work in factories. Many more were recent immigrants, a lot of whom did not speak English well, if at all. Such people were likely to live in dreadful slums, where families of four or five people might have two-room apartments in disease-ridden tenements, sharing one toilet with other families.

The plight of the "have-nots" made an impression on young Eleanor. She later wrote, "Very early I became conscious of the fact that there were people around me who suffered in one way or another." She recalled the first time she saw how the poor lived:

> *I was five or six when my father took me to help serve Thanksgiving dinner in one of the newsboys' clubhouses. . . . My father explained that many of these ragged little boys had no homes and lived in little wooden shanties in empty lots, or slept in vestibules [lobbies] of houses or public buildings or any place where they could be moderately warm. . . .*

At the top of the ladder was a tiny handful of very rich people who lived in grand houses and had many servants. There were such people in most American cities, but the high-society group in New York was particularly celebrated as "The Four Hundred"—meaning the top wealthiest four hundred families in the city. Such people knew one another, married one another, went to one anothers' weddings and parties, met one another at the

Eleanor stands with her father, the charming but incompetent Elliott Roosevelt, in their country house on Long Island, near New York City. A groom holds the horse. Elliott was a great horseman and polo player.

opera, at polo matches, at horse shows. Most of its members came from "old money"—that is, their families had been wealthy for several generations. The Four Hundred considered themselves "ladies and gentlemen," an American elite, who were better than everybody else.

Getting into the Four Hundred was not easy, and if you were not careful about what you did, you might be cut out of it. For women life was particularly confining. They could not marry anyone lower on the social scale, but had to marry someone from high society.

They had to go to the right parties and give parties to which only the right people were invited. They always had to behave politely and decorously. They could not laugh raucously or wave their arms around to make a point. Children could not bounce around the house, roughhousing and yelling. Women could not sit with their legs crossed. Young people certainly could not go on dates. Indeed, an unmarried woman could not be seen in public alone with a single man unless he was her brother or another close relative. Society women could not work, except at charity. Few women became doctors, went into business, or ran for public office.

Anna Roosevelt expected her daughter, Eleanor, to become such a woman. Anna was fond of her children, but she was strict about the rules of society. She did not want her children to disgrace her by trying to have careers or by marrying the wrong sort of person.

Thus, Eleanor was taught French and German from an early age, so she would be able to converse with wealthy Europeans of her own class. She was supposed to know a little something about music and art, a little Latin and Greek. But mainly she had to learn how to manage a houseful of servants, how to give elaborate dinner parties, how to make conversation with the often boring people she met at other women's dinner parties.

Eleanor was a dutiful child, and she did learn all these things. In fact, she became quite fluent in French, which proved to be helpful later on when she was meeting world leaders. But it was a very rigid life for a child and could not have made Eleanor happy.

She soon had a baby brother, Elliott Jr., whom she liked taking care of. "Eleanor is so sweet and good" with him, her father said. It was her father, the handsome and charming Elliott Roosevelt, who was the great love and solace of Eleanor's life.

Eleanor with her beloved father. Her brother, Elliott, Jr., is on the right, her brother Hall on the left. Elliott, Jr., died young.

Once, when Eleanor and her father took a trip to Venice, Italy, they spent hours together wandering along the canals, and feeding the pigeons in St. Mark's Square. When they went out on the canal in one of Venice's famous gondolas, she laughed and clapped as her father pretended to be one of the gondoliers who poled the boat along, and sang along with the gondoliers.

Her father often read to Eleanor. "I had a special interest in *The Old Curiosity Shop* [by Charles Dickens] because my father used to call me 'Little Nell' after the child in the story and I first learned to care for Longfellow's poems because my father was devoted to 'Hiawatha.'" At the age of eight she learned almost all of the long poem to surprise her father.

By this time Elliott was beginning to show signs of his heavy drinking and unreliability. But Eleanor was his favorite, and he tried to see her when he was able to do so. Hall sits on one knee.

Unfortunately, despite his intelligence and charm, Elliott Roosevelt was a troubled person underneath. Although the men of high society did not have to work, many of them did, but Elliott was never able to hold down a job for very long. Even when Eleanor was a child, he drank too much and began spending a lot of time away from his family with his cronies. He became increasingly unreliable. He would disappear for days at a time, and then reappear, begging his family for forgiveness.

Sometimes he became violent and shouted in a threatening way. At times he seemed to be losing his mind. Three times he threatened to kill himself.

By 1891, Anna Roosevelt could take it no longer. She had just had another baby, a boy named Hall. Fearful for the safety of her children, she asked Elliott to leave. From this time on, Eleanor's beloved father was in and out of her life.

Anna Roosevelt had often been ill. In November 1892 she had to have an operation. A month later, she came down with a bad infectious disease called diphtheria and died. Anna had made her own mother, not Elliott, the guardian of the children. Not long after Anna died, Elliott came to visit Eleanor. She later wrote:

> *He was dressed all in black, looking very sad. He held out his arms and gathered me to him. In a little while he began to talk. . . . Someday . . . we would travel together and do many things which he painted as interesting and pleasant. Somehow it was always he and I. . . . There started that day a feeling which never left me, that he and I were very close and someday would have a life of our own together.*

Taking his promises to heart, young Eleanor withdrew into a fantasy world "in which I was the heroine and my father the hero." But Elliott continued to be as unreliable as ever. Sometimes he would visit her, sometimes he wouldn't. Sometimes he answered her letters, sometimes he didn't. When Eleanor was eight years old, her father once came to visit and took her for a walk. After a bit they went to his club. Elliott left Eleanor there with the doorman. After six hours, when Elliott had not returned, the doorman took Eleanor home. To be abandoned like that was a harsh experience for a young child. In 1894, her father died of the effects of alcohol. Despite everything, for the rest of her life Eleanor continued to think fondly of her father and remembered him often.

Another formal portrait of Eleanor and her father

On top of everything, in the years between her mother's and father's deaths, her brother Elliott died. She had seen enough tragedy. She and her baby brother, Hall, were now living in their grandmother's large dark house in New York City. Her grandmother was kind, but she was busy with other members of her family and had little time for Eleanor. The children were put in the care of a nanny who was cruel to Eleanor. She pulled her hair when she did something wrong. The shy girl did not dare tell her grandmother about the nanny until she was much older. Later, a cousin who was around at the time said about the nanny, "She was a terrifying character." Because of the nanny and the general gloom of the house, few of Eleanor's friends wanted to visit her. "There was no place to play games, unbroken gloom everywhere," the cousin said. "We ate our suppers in silence. . . . It was the grimmest childhood I have ever known. Who did she have? Nobody."

Then suddenly everything changed. As she reached fifteen, her grandmother decided that Eleanor needed more education than she was getting at home. She also felt that it would do the teenager good to get away from the family for awhile, which was undoubtedly true. People in high society often

Later, Eleanor said that some of the best years of her life were spent at Allenswood, a school in England. The headmistress of the school took an interest in her, and she blossomed. In this photo, students pose in front of the grand school buildings, once the home of a British aristocrat.

sent their children to school in Europe. Some of Eleanor's relatives had gone to a school in England called Allenswood, run by a Frenchwoman named Mademoiselle (Mlle.) Marie Souvestre. So Eleanor was sent there.

She got off to a good start. At Allenswood the girls were expected to speak French at meals. Eleanor had been learning French from infancy and already spoke it well. One fellow student said that at her first dinner at the school, "When we hardly dared open our mouths, she sat opposite Mlle. Souvestre chatting away in French . . . we admired her courage."

As it turned out, Mlle. Souvestre was not as concerned about the rules and regulations of high society as the people back in New York had been. She encouraged her students to be imaginative, to take an interest in modern ideas, literature, and the arts. Mlle. Souvestre began to open the world to Eleanor. In particular, she showed Eleanor that a woman did not have to devote her life to keeping up with society, but could strike out on her own and do interesting things. One writer who knew Eleanor well said, "Mlle. Souvestre was the most influential figure in Eleanor's early years, second only to her father. Headmistress and pupil were strongly drawn to each other." A cousin of Eleanor's who was also attending Allenswood at that time said that Mlle. Souvestre became interested in Eleanor because she realized that "she could give a great deal to that really remarkable, sad young girl."

Mlle. Souvestre's support helped bring out Eleanor's best qualities. Following Eleanor's first year at Allenswood, Mlle. Souvestre wrote to Eleanor's grandmother back in New York:

> *She is full of sympathy for those who live with her and shows an intelligent interest in everything she comes in contact with. . . . As a pupil she is very satisfactory, but even that is of small account when you compare it with the perfect quality of her soul.*

Eleanor soon became one of the most popular girls in the school, a star. It was a strange but happy feeling for her. When she came home from the school in England at the age of eighteen, she was a different person. She was still somewhat shy, but she was much more confident than she had been before her stay in England. Those three years at Allenswood were the happiest time of her life.

Chapter 2

THE FATEFUL MARRIAGE

A CHILD GROWING UP WITH SUCH gloom and so much death—feeling not good enough for her mother and wondering when her father would come to visit—was bound to be affected. Her mother and a brother had died when she was eight, and her father when she was almost ten. At the time Eleanor had nobody she could really count on for affection

In Eleanor's day, young women in society were presented at a large ball each year. This ball meant that they were old enough to marry. Eleanor "came out" as expected, but instead of taking up society life, she followed a different path. This is her coming out photograph.

and support. As a result, she felt like an underdog. Increasingly through her life she would take up the cause of the poor, the sick, and the weary. She wrote, "The feeling that I was useful was perhaps the greatest joy I experienced. . . . The surest way to be happy is to seek happiness for others." This idea would become the great rule of her life.

Eleanor did not plan to go to college. Although some young women did attend college, it was not usual at that time. She could now have done what most of her society friends were doing—go to parties, the opera, and dances in order to meet the right sort of young man to marry. But she was coming to understand that she did not want that sort of life. So she joined a group of a few other wealthy women who were working with what were called "settlement houses."

Settlement houses existed in many cities. In the years around 1900 vast numbers of immigrants were flooding into the United States from Europe and to some extent elsewhere. They often found themselves in difficulties. They worked at low-paying jobs, did not speak English, and had problems adjusting to their new home. The settlement houses were set up to educate the immigrants in American ways and to help them out generally.

Eleanor began teaching dance and other classes at the Rivington Street settlement house on the lower east side of Manhattan. This was the heart of New York's immigrant area, and Eleanor loved working there. More important, it was her first real experience with the "have-nots" of America. She got to know young girls who worked in factories for twelve or more hours a day, six days a week, for six dollars a week in pay.

Rivington Street in New York City's lower east side was a typical crowded slum. People, mostly immigrants, were crammed into small apartments and spent much of their time on the street. As Eleanor quickly discovered, the lives of these poor people were far different from those of her friends and family.

Eleanor also joined the Consumers League, a group trying to improve working conditions in the cities. She was asked to investigate sweatshops, where many young children worked, making artificial flowers and the like. The sweatshops were located in tenement homes instead of factory buildings. So Eleanor went into dirty, disease-ridden slums, climbed six flights of stairs to visit children living four to a room, who were often hungry. She was "appalled" by what she discovered. "I saw little children of four and five [working] at tables until they dropped from fatigue." It was the start of a long life of making herself "useful" to people in need.

Something else was happening in her life that would have great importance not only for her, but to the history of the United States. Eleanor was seeing a young man about her age, her distant cousin, Franklin Delano Roosevelt.

Like Eleanor, Franklin came from New York society. He was wealthy, handsome, and charming. He was fun-loving, as he would always be. He liked nothing better than to get together with a few pals to play poker and talk. He loved the sea and for most of his life had his own yacht. Many people thought he was a "lightweight"—not serious enough to do important work. But underneath, Franklin Roosevelt had great ambition.

Eleanor with Franklin Roosevelt not long after they married. They are at Franklin's mother's large estate in Hyde Park, New York. Living under the command of her domineering mother-in-law was hard for Eleanor, but she always managed to keep the peace.

Franklin and Eleanor began to see more and more of each other. Soon Eleanor fell in love with Franklin. Historians have long wondered why the very serious Eleanor and the cheerful, fun-loving Franklin chose each other. It is true that most young women of the time would have considered the wealthy, good-looking Franklin a very good "catch." Perhaps Eleanor was flattered that this young man, who many other women in her group wanted, had chosen her.

For Franklin's part, he admired Eleanor for her intelligence, her reliability, her thoughtfulness, and her insights into other people. He had ambitions: there was his cousin Ted already in the White House. Perhaps he realized that Eleanor was the sort of woman who could be counted on to help him get where he wanted to go.

There was one other thing. As it turned out, Franklin also did not want to spend his life living by the rules of society. He wanted to do more interesting things and involve himself with all sorts of people. It was something they shared.

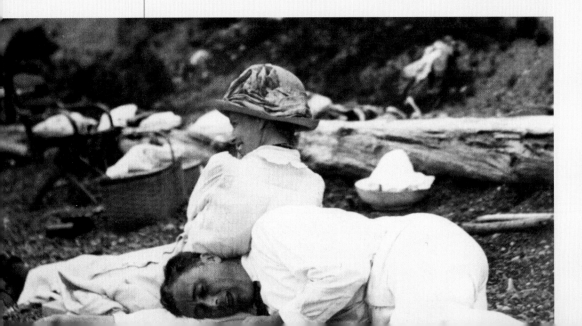

Eleanor and Franklin relax at their rural vacation home, Campobello.

However, Franklin's mother, Sara, did not approve of the possible marriage. Her husband, Franklin's father, had died a few years earlier. In her sorrow, Sara had drawn her son close to her. She didn't want him to marry at all. She wanted Franklin to spend his life with her, living at their grand estate in Hyde Park on the Hudson River in upstate New York.

Throughout his life Franklin remained close to his mother, which would frequently be a problem for Eleanor. But he did not take orders from her. He was determined to marry Eleanor, and in March 1905, they were wed. The president of the United States, Eleanor's "Uncle Ted," came to the wedding and stole the show.

Eleanor decided that her first job was to please her energetic husband and to somehow get along with her domineering mother-in-law. Children began coming quickly, the first one in 1906. Franklin was finishing his law degree. They were living in New York City, but they spent most holidays at Sara's Hyde Park estate. Here Sara, not Eleanor, was boss of the family. The Roosevelts also owned a grand summer home at Campobello, an island off Canada close to Maine. They would spend summers there.

Eleanor in the Hyde Park house with three of her children: James, Elliott, named for her father, and Anna, named for her mother. Even though Eleanor spent much of her life working for the poor, she always lived in great comfort, as this photo shows.

Eleanor had to not only take care of her growing family, but also to move them frequently among New York City, Hyde Park, and Campobello. On top of it, Franklin liked having company and was always inviting friends and business associates for lunch and dinner. Of course they had servants. Still, managing this sort of establishment was a big job.

Franklin soon earned his law degree, but he had no intention of becoming a lawyer. His heart was set on politics. Most wealthy people of that time were Republicans. Eleanor's celebrated uncle, Teddy Roosevelt, was a Republican, as were most of her family. But Franklin's side were Democrats, and Eleanor loyally decided to become a Democrat. As it turned out, the policies of the Democratic party suited her own ideas best.

In 1910 Franklin ran for state senator in the upstate New York district around Hyde Park. The people there were strongly Republican, but the handsome young Franklin Roosevelt charmed them, and he won

Eleanor (second from left), with some friends at Campobello. The car, with a convertible top, was very fashionable for the time.

Franklin at a political gathering in upstate New York at the time he was running for state senator. Even though he came from a wealthy and social background, he was always able to get along with people of all kinds. In this photo, we can see his famous smile and charming manner.

by a big margin. Officials of the Democratic party took notice that he was a vote getter.

Many members of the state legislature did not live in Albany, the state capital, but came only for meetings. Franklin, however, decided that he wanted to be close to the political talk and events. So they moved to Albany. Suddenly the shy Eleanor Roosevelt found herself the wife of a public man. People were constantly coming to the house for lunch, dinner, tea, conversations in the evening. Eleanor began to learn politics from the inside. She liked being with people, but she did not enjoy political maneuvering as much as her husband did. She would, however, become very good at it.

In 1912 a Democrat, Woodrow Wilson, was elected president. Franklin wanted a job with the new administration in Washington. In particular, he wanted to become assistant secretary of the navy. He had always loved ships and the sea. But more than that, his older cousin Ted had held the job on his way to the White House. Franklin got the appointment, and the Roosevelts moved to Washington, D.C.

Franklin, when he was assistant secretary of the navy, with some of the most famous men of his day. William Jennings Bryan, one of the foremost politicians of the time, is wearing a white suit. President Woodrow Wilson is in a black jacket and white pants. Roosevelt is at the right.

As it turned out, it was a more important job than anyone had expected. World War I broke out in Europe in 1914, and by 1916 American was getting its own army ready to fight, just in case. In 1917 America joined the war. Franklin was now an important official in the American war effort.

In wartime Washington, Eleanor was drawn even deeper into politics. She was constantly entertaining important people, like the British ambassador and Supreme Court justices. But, like many Americans, she also did volunteer work. She joined the Red Cross and helped set up canteens that served soup, coffee, and sandwiches to soldiers coming into Washington on troop trains. She would sometimes go to her canteen at five in the morning. She was also in charge of a volunteer knitting program for the navy, that organized women to knit socks and sweaters for sailors.

World War I ended in victory for the American side. For Eleanor its effects would last a lifetime. She had had a brief fling at public service during her time with the settlement houses. The wartime work with the Red Cross and the navy had shown her that serving others in this way made her feel worthwhile, like a person of value. No longer was she the shy ugly duckling of her childhood. Nor was she simply the wife of a public official helping to entertain important people. She was a person in her own right, with real jobs to do. One of her biographers wrote, "She would never again be content with purely private satisfactions, and for the rest of her life she would look at the injustices of the world, feel pity for the human condition, and ask what she could do about it."

Chapter 3

TRAGEDY STRIKES

IN 1920 THE REPUBLICANS WON BACK the White House. As was customary, the Democratic officials resigned and were replaced by Republican ones. The Roosevelts went back to New York, and Franklin joined a law firm. However, he had made a mark as a promising candidate for office. He got into various public activities and looked around for his next step upward.

Eleanor as a young wife in a quiet moment

Eleanor, too, was looking around. She had come to see that a life in politics meant Franklin would be spending a lot of time away from her at meetings or traveling to talk to voters. She was determined to have an interesting life of her own. But opportunities for women were still limited. Women were not welcome in business offices, although occasionally one broke through. A few women had become lawyers and doctors, but not many. Women were almost never chosen to run for public office.

But in truth, women had made great progress since the time Eleanor was growing up. A major breakthrough came in 1920, when women were at last allowed to vote. Women were feeling confident that they could make more progress in the years to come.

Eleanor decided to join a new organization called the League of Women Voters. The idea of the league was to make sure that women used the vote they had just gotten wisely. Eleanor Roosevelt had previous experience in politics. She was intelligent and not afraid to assert herself when she felt she was doing the right thing. Very quickly the leaders of the organization saw her value, and she soon had her hands full.

In 1920, American women were able to vote in a presidential election for the first time. The newly formed League of Women Voters urged women to make good use of the vote. Eleanor, a leading member of the organization, stands at a voting machine. In reality, she would have had the curtain closed to conceal her vote.

For the Roosevelts, the future looked bright. Franklin was planning to run for the governorship of New York state. Eleanor had her work with the League of Women Voters, and would also help in Franklin's campaign.

In the summer of 1921 they went as usual to the vacation house on the island of Campobello. Here Franklin could sail his yacht, work on his stamp collection, and consult with his advisors about the campaign for the governorship. All was well.

On July 30 Eleanor thought that Franklin looked tired. But with his usual irrepressible spirits, he went for a cruise. A few days later, however, he felt "dull." Still, on August 10 he helped to put out a small forest fire he had spotted from his yacht. He still felt tired, and he took a quick swim in the cold water in hopes of perking himself up. The swim did not help much. He went to bed early that night.

The next morning he felt worse. When he got out of bed he realized that there was something wrong with his left leg. Soon he was unable to move it. By afternoon his temperature had soared to 102 degrees, and his right leg had become useless. By the next day he was paralyzed from the waist down. Doctors came. At first it was thought that the paralysis was due to a blood clot on his spine. But in the back of everybody's mind was the thought of the dreaded infantile paralysis, today known as polio.

This disease had existed for a long time, but it was victimizing more and more Americans. There had been a bad outbreak of polio in 1916. By the early 1920s it was cropping up regularly every summer, particularly in cities. It especially affected children and teenagers— which is why it was called *infantile* paralysis—but, as in Franklin's case, it sometimes struck adults as well.

In some cases the patient suffered pain and mild paralysis for a few days, then got well. In other cases the patient died. But in a great many cases the sick person was left partly paralyzed. It might leave the patient with just a slight limp. Some victims, especially children, were left paralyzed from the neck down. Polio was a terrible disease. Today, due to polio vaccines, it has been largely stamped out. But in any community we still occasionally see its victims, men and women in their fifties and older wearing leg braces from the polio they had when they were young.

Soon the doctors agreed that Franklin did indeed have polio. Now Eleanor had not only a large family and her own work to manage, but also a desperately sick husband to care for. She bathed him, massaged his useless legs, helped him to sit up, cheered him up. Slowly his temperature went back to normal. But he still could not move his legs.

Franklin was sure he would in time completely recover. His old cheerfulness returned. Eleanor knew better. More doctors were called in. They brought the invalid back to New York, where he was hospitalized. He tried special exercises. His legs began to bend closed and lock. They were put in casts to hold them straight. The pain was terrible. Grimly, Franklin endured.

Slowly the pain ebbed, and the time came when Franklin Roosevelt was able to start using a wheelchair. He now considered taking up his old activities.

It was several years before Franklin really gave up the idea that he might walk again. He was always hoping that a new medicine or a different exercise would improve his legs. Later on, he discovered that paddling around in warm water seemed to help a little, and he started a place for polio sufferers in Warm Springs, Georgia, where naturally warm water spurted from the ground. As president, he visited Warm Springs often.

Franklin at Warm Springs, Georgia, where he was creating a recuperation home for victims of polio, or infantile paralysis, as it was called then. Roosevelt only allowed himself to be photographed in ways that made him appear healthy, as in this shot. But he could not actually walk and could only stand with help.

But, in fact, his legs never got better. During his long political career he always needed help standing. He tried not to let people see how crippled he was. He rarely let photographers take pictures of him in a wheelchair, instead he was always sitting behind his desk or in an ordinary easy chair. Sometimes, with his braces locked in place and somebody beside him for support, he could stand long enough to make a brief speech. But he would live out his life in a wheelchair. He had a little car fitted with hand controls which he could drive around the Hyde Park estate, but he could not drive a regular car on roads and highways. He could not really swim, he could only paddle around. Nor could he go for long walks in the woods, or play rough-and-tumble games with his children.

The effects of polio on Franklin Roosevelt were not just physical. He changed mentally as well. He had suffered much pain and loss. He understood better how people who life had treated hard must feel. He was no longer the "lightweight" many people had thought him to be. His sympathy for the poor, the ill, and the deprived grew. As president, he would become the champion of "the forgotten man," as he once put it, against the rich and powerful. He had now joined Eleanor in the desire to help the underdog.

Once it was clear that Franklin's paralysis would not be cured quickly, if ever, both of them had to accept and adjust. Franklin began thinking about a return to politics. Eleanor plunged back into her work. She kept on with the League of Women Voters. She also joined another group called the Women's Trade Union League.

As we have seen, in those days ordinary workers—the majority of Americans—found life to be very hard. Most worked ten or twelve hours a day, six days a week, for low pay. There were no medical plans. Many people could not afford to see a doctor or buy medicines when they were sick. There was no Social Security, no unemployment insurance. If you lost your job you would have to beg help from friends and relatives, who often had little enough themselves. There were no pension plans. When you got too old to work you had to count on your children to support you—if they could. Unfortunately, many of the people who ran companies believed they could not make profits unless wages were kept low. They would not raise wages or even provide drinking fountains, clean washrooms, much less coffee breaks, unless they were forced to.

The only weapons workers had against "the bosses," as they were often called, were their unions.

If the workers in a factory got together in a union and threatened to call a strike, they might force the managers of the factory to improve things. But for the workers it was a very hard struggle. Sometimes the factory managers would bring in "strikebreakers" to replace the striking workers. Other times government officials interfered on the side of the factory owners to force the strikers back to work. For many decades, labor conflicts had frequently ended in violence.

This photo shows women in a factory in 1918. Before Franklin Roosevelt's New Deal, most American workers labored long hours in poor conditions for low pay. Eleanor strongly supported the workers and their unions and encouraged Franklin to fight for workers' rights.

In throwing herself into the union movement, Eleanor Roosevelt was going directly against the society people she had grown up with, including members of her own family—some of her cousins, aunts, and uncles. The wealth of such people came mainly from the profits from industry. The lower the wages could be kept, the greater those profits would be. Indeed, if wages were raised, Franklin and Eleanor's own income might be hurt. (In fact, in the long term it worked out the other way around. Stronger unions would help to create great prosperity in America later on, which benefited the rich as well as the working people.)

Eleanor did not care if her society friends were disturbed by her union work. She plunged in. Gradually her old friends from high society fell away. Her new friends were quite different. These were often fiery, determined women who wanted to improve things for the workers. Rose Schneiderman was a "redheaded packet of social dynamite," who had immigrated from Poland and still spoke with an accent. Maud Swartz had helped to organize unions in England. Such people were very different from the wealthy girls Eleanor had gone to school with. But to Eleanor they were part of an exciting world that was new to her. From them she learned about the importance of unions.

She brought them home to talk to her husband about union work. Eleanor and Franklin were growing away from the privileged life they had been born into.

Franklin was now back into politics. In 1928 there would be elections. However, it did not seem like a good moment for the Democrats. During the 1920s the country had been going through a period of what seemed to be great prosperity. The stock market had raced upward, and many people seemed to be getting rich buying and selling stocks. Actually, the prosperity was hollow. The fact was workers were badly under-paid, and businesses were not doing as well as many people thought. But in 1928 few people realized that. Americans seemed to be growing richer day by day, and the Republicans, who controlled the government, were getting the credit. Nonetheless, Franklin was persuaded to run for the governorship of New York.

The Democrats fought hard, but as most people expected, their candidate for president lost. But Roosevelt did win the governor's office. It was clear that he was growing very popular with the voters. Would he run for president in 1932?

In the fall of 1929 he had not yet decided. Then suddenly, the stock market raced downward faster than it had gone up. The great prosperity of the 1920s

It is difficult for Americans today to imagine the poverty and despair of the Great Depression. This photograph, taken in 1934, shows children playing with garbage for lack of anything better to do. Many children did not have shoes, much less bicycles and baseball gloves.

vanished overnight. Factories closed, and people lost their jobs. Hundreds of banks closed for good, so that millions of Americans lost all their savings. By the early 1930s there were times when a quarter of all workers had no jobs. The Great Depression of the 1930s had begun.

Poverty stalked the land. Children who had once lived in nice houses with plenty of toys found themselves struggling to earn money for a pair of shoes—if they could find a job. Thousands became homeless and picked through garbage cans for supper. Shacktowns grew up by railroad tracks and at the edges of towns. Kids as young as ten and twelve wandered the streets on their own, many of them girls dressed as boys.

By the election of 1932 America was in despair. Inevitably, the Republican president, Herbert Hoover, was blamed, although it was not his fault. And so the people turned to the warm, optimistic Franklin D. Roosevelt. In March 1933, Eleanor Roosevelt found herself living in the White House.

Chapter 4

FIRST LADY

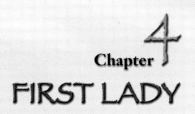

HISTORIANS HAVE LONG ARGUED about the influence of Eleanor Roosevelt on Franklin during the years he was president. It is a very complicated question. For one thing, it is clear that for some time Eleanor and Franklin had grown somewhat apart. Both were independent-minded people. Each had their own circle of friends and their own work. This is not surprising, for they were in many ways different types of people.

A formal portrait of Eleanor during her early days in the White House. While she could dress and behave elegantly, she was happiest when meeting with ordinary people and working at the causes she believed in. Fancy clothes and lavish meals meant little to her.

Eleanor was serious, always trying to be useful and do things for other people. Franklin, too, had his serious side and a concern for other people, but he was basically a cheerful man who liked to have his fun when he got the chance. There were times when he did not want Eleanor telling him what his duty was.

Nonetheless, Franklin admired Eleanor enormously. He respected her intelligence and her good sense. And often enough, when she pointed out to him some injustice, he did something about it. And when, for political reasons, he could not or would not do what she suggested, she would quietly accept it. They were, then, more like partners in a common cause. So it is hard to say exactly how much Eleanor influenced Franklin. But she was always there at dinnertime to quietly remind him of things, and she fell into the habit of passing along to him notes and letters about matters she wanted him to consider. Had she not been there, it is probable that Franklin would not have worked as much as he did to help the deprived in America.

And there were plenty of deprived people, partly because of the Depression, and partly for other reasons. Franklin Roosevelt came to the White House promising a "new deal" for Americans. Ever since then his programs have been called the New Deal.

Eleanor and Franklin relaxing at Hyde Park, shortly after Franklin became president. Once again, Franklin is shown seated, without his wheelchair. Hyde Park is open to the public now, and is a fascinating place for students of the Roosevelts to visit.

Put simply, the New Deal was an effort to use the federal government to help people who were in trouble, which during the Depression was perhaps half of all Americans. For some time before this, many people had believed in keeping government small. Things would work best if the government stayed out of the way. But in the Depression, it was clear that things were barely working at all. Americans were demanding that the government step in and fix things.

This is often the case. Most people are against government interference except when it benefits them. For instance, few Americans want the government to stop delivering the mail, to give up Social Security and

Medicare, to stop programs for schools and roads. Indeed, millions of Americans today are strongly urging the government to interfere in matters like the environment and other issues.

As president, Franklin Roosevelt had little choice but to bring the government into the lives of ordinary people. In the end he pushed through many programs that we consider essential today, like Social Security, protections for labor unions, and many kinds of regulations to make sure businesses are fair to workers and customers.

These New Deal programs were exactly the sorts of policies that Eleanor favored. But for Eleanor, things were always personal. Where Franklin thought in terms of ideas and policies, Eleanor was touched by individual people whose stories tugged at her heart. She always received a flood of letters from people asking her for help. Most of them had to be answered by her small staff, especially Malvina Thompson, always known as Tommy, who devoted her life to Eleanor. But she personally answered letters that touched her. One was from a poor young woman named Bertha Brodsky, whose father was struggling to support his family with a newspaper route. Bertha's back was deformed. Eleanor arranged for her to be operated on, visited her in the hospital, sent her Christmas packages, and eventually went to her wedding. Bertha called her a "messenger of God." She was only one of many people Eleanor helped.

But Eleanor Roosevelt was not content to work behind the scenes, prodding her husband and helping the forlorn. Almost as soon as she moved into the White House she began holding press conferences. No other First Lady had done this. At the beginning these press conferences were only for women reporters. They covered matters thought to be of interest to women like what sort of meals Eleanor served the president and their guests and how she was raising her children (she still had two teenagers at home).

But as time went on Eleanor began to talk more and more about national issues she thought important. She spoke out against child labor, for increases to teachers' salaries, for better conditions for women workers. She tried, through her press conferences, to teach American housewives how to prepare nutritious meals during times when money was short. She publicized a "7-cent luncheon" she had served at the White House—hot stuffed eggs with tomato sauce, mashed potatoes, prune pudding, bread, and coffee—at the time this was considered a good, inexpensive meal.

Anyone who studies the life of Eleanor Roosevelt must be struck by the extraordinary amount of energy and resilience she had. She was always up at 7:30 in the morning and if not earlier. She would exercise or ride her horse in Rock Creek Park. She rarely took more than a brief break during the course of the day, going from one meeting to the next, holding press

Eleanor with her daughter Anna and one of her grandchildren. She asked her grandchildren to visit as often as they could.

conferences, seeing officials. She usually had important people or government officials to lunch and dinner, so she could get them to see her point on issues she was interested in. She was, of course, careful not to go against Franklin's policies for the government. Her usual way was to talk to Franklin about something that concerned her. If he agreed with her she would invite the right official to lunch and argue her case. If Franklin didn't want her to push a certain point, she would hold off until a better time. And on top of this, for most of the remainder of her life she wrote a daily newspaper column, "My Day," frequently dictating it to Tommy late at night after a hectic day.

Of course she remained a wife, a mother, and now a grandmother. She installed a nursery on the third floor of the White House for her grandchildren and a sandbox and jungle gym on the lawn for playtime.

She had dogs and often walked them at night herself, although she could easily have had someone else walk them. It seemed to many Americans that Eleanor Roosevelt was everywhere. Some resented her. They felt that a proper First Lady should stay home and take care of her family. But most approved. Eleanor, in any case, did not care what anyone thought. She would always reach out to help people.

One cause that increasingly concerned her was civil rights for African Americans. At the time, most white Americans were prejudiced against blacks. Few had any black friends or wanted them. Blacks had great difficulty being accepted at most colleges, could not get office jobs in businesses, and usually had to work at the lowest-paying jobs, no matter how smart they were. Worse, in the South blacks were sometimes lynched, whether they had done anything wrong or not.

Very early in her years as First Lady, Eleanor invited a group of black leaders to visit her at the White House to discuss racial problems. It was, said one person who was there, "a memorable evening." For the first time African Americans felt that somebody in the White House was listening to them. Soon Eleanor spoke out about the poor quality of schools for blacks, especially in the South.

In particular, she urged Franklin to do something about the lynching of African Americans. It was a hard thing for him to do, because Southerners controlled much of the Senate and would not permit a federal law against lynching to pass. But Eleanor would not give up. She visited African-American colleges and schools, sometimes riding to them in cars with blacks, which many whites would not have done. She wanted "to give Negroes the feeling that they were not alone." (*Negro* was then the accepted term for African American.) She kept on trying, but with so many Americans unwilling to accept blacks as equals, she made little progress.

Eleanor Roosevelt visits a nursery school that had been created by one of Franklin's New Deal programs. She poured a huge amount of time and energy into programs like this one. She was especially concerned about rights for African Americans.

But by opening the White House to blacks she sent a message to other Americans that would in time help to change their minds.

Meanwhile, the Depression continued. Nothing Franklin Roosevelt tried seemed to do much good, although certainly New Deal programs reduced a lot of suffering. Nonetheless, people had faith in Franklin and in 1936 elected him for a second term.

By now foreign problems were looming. In Europe fascist dictators were taking over—Hitler in Germany, Mussolini in Italy, Franco in Spain. These dictators were not only oppressing their own people, they were trying to move into neighboring lands. The democratic nations, like England and France, were slow to stand up to these dictators. With the pain of World War I fresh in everybody's mind, nobody wanted to risk another war. Nonetheless, in 1939 World War II began, with France and England against Germany and Italy. Later the Russians were drawn in against Hitler, too. Through these years Franklin became ever more certain that eventually the United States would have to join the fighting. But Americans were not ready for another war and wanted to stay out of it.

Still, most Americans sympathized with England and France—the Allies as they were called. After the

Germans took France, Franklin gave England what help he was able to. Eleanor had always been a pacifist, opposed to war. But she began to see that the fascists had to be stopped.

One of the best-known incidents in Eleanor's life came shortly before the start of the war. The president had asked the king and queen of England to visit the United States. Eleanor of course had to arrange various receptions and dinner parties for the royal couple. One of these was a big picnic at the Hyde Park estate. Eleanor served the king and queen hot dogs.

The newspapers made a big story out of it. Many people felt that serving hot dogs to royalty was impolite, but most Americans thought it was a wonderful idea. It was just what Eleanor would do to show that in American democracy one person was as good as the next.

In 1940 there would be another presidential election. The first president, George Washington, had refused to run for a third term, which he could have easily won. Ever since, it had been the custom for presidents to serve for only two terms. As the new election came closer, Franklin wondered what to do. In his heart he wanted to continue as president. The New Deal had not yet ended the Depression, and the country was probably going to be at war soon. But it would break with long-standing custom for him to run again.

If there had been available a strong Democratic candidate to carry out his New Deal ideas, Franklin might have stepped aside. But there was no such person, so the Democrats insisted that he run. At the Democratic convention in Chicago he was nominated.

Franklin wanted his secretary of agriculture, Henry Wallace, to run for vice president. It was an important choice, for everybody knew that a man of Franklin's age might die in office.

Franklin stayed away from the convention, as was the custom. But he wanted Eleanor to be there. There was much opposition to Wallace. Every time his name was mentioned there was, says one biographer, "a roar of boos and catcalls." It was decided that Eleanor must speak. She said that the next president faced "a heavier responsibility, perhaps, than any man has ever faced before in this country. . . . No man who is a candidate or who is President can carry this situation alone. This is only carried by a united people who love their country."

According to the biographer, "As she finished, the hall was absolutely still. Petty rancors and rivalries had visibly subsided, and for the moment the convention was united." As Franklin had wished, Wallace received the nomination.

At the 1940 Democratic Convention Eleanor gave a powerful speech in support of Franklin's choice for vice president. Because the delegates to the convention believed in her honesty, they came around to Franklin's side.

Why had Eleanor succeeded with a brief speech, where all the powerful politicians at the convention had failed? It was because everybody knew that Eleanor Roosevelt, more than anyone there, wanted nothing for herself. She was only thinking of her country.

In truth, Eleanor did not want to stay in the White House. No matter how independent she is, a First Lady has a great many duties—people she must be nice to, receptions to attend, state dinners to manage. But Eleanor knew that she must stay on if the people wanted Franklin. And they did; he was elected to a third term.

A year later the war they had expected came. The Japanese bombed the American naval base at Pearl Harbor in Hawaii and marched into other areas around the Pacific, determined to build an empire for themselves. The United States was now in World War II.

Eleanor was busier during the war than she had ever been. She was particularly interested in helping the refugees trying to run from Europe. Many Jews were fleeing in hopes of escaping Hitler's death camps. Tens of thousands of children had lost their parents and needed to find safety. People who opposed the dictators would be executed if they could not get away. Eleanor tried to help as many of these people as she could.

Equally important, she was asked to travel around the world to wherever American men were fighting to show them that they had not been forgotten by their government. She went all over the Pacific area, visiting hospitals full of wounded men, some missing arms and legs. She did not come to the door of a hospital ward and say a few words. Instead, she stopped at every bed, spoke to every man, and frequently took messages from the men to give to their families at home. She traveled in jeeps, visited battle zones, went to bed in a little cot at midnight, and got up at five to visit more soldiers.

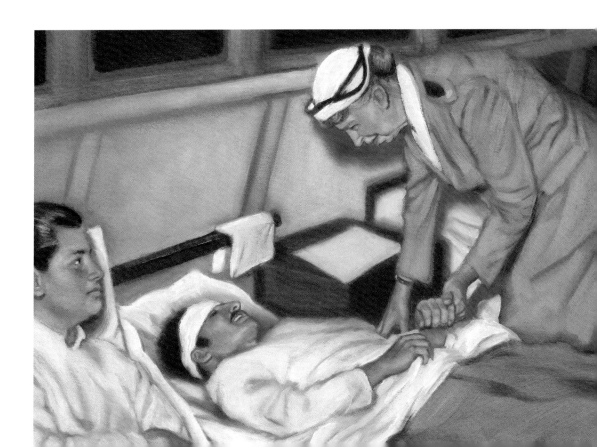

While the men were always excited and pleased to see her, some of the top officers were not. The famous Admiral William "Bull" Halsey was particularly annoyed to have her around. He was trying to win a war and had no time to spare for her, nor troops to look after her. By the time Eleanor left, Admiral Halsey had changed his tune.

During World War II, Eleanor often flew to combat zones to talk to the troops. She showed them that they were not forgotten at home. The war was far more deadly than any war we have had since. Many of the young men she met would be wounded or killed. Here, Eleanor talks to sailors on the Pacific island of Bora Bora.

He said, "I marveled at her hardihood, both physical and mental. She walked for miles, and she saw patients who were grievously and gruesomely wounded. But I marveled most at their expressions as she leaned over them. It was a sight I will never forget." And he added later, "She alone accomplished more good than any other person, or any group of civilians, who had passed through my area."

But despite the war, Eleanor had it in mind that the New Deal had made promises to people that had to be kept. One of the president's most important advisors, Harry Hopkins, reported about a talk Eleanor had with Hopkins and Franklin. "She impressed upon us both," Hopkins said, that the president was "under moral obligation to see his domestic reforms through . . . in such a way as to give everybody a job." She had become "the keeper of and constant spokesman for her husband's conscience."

By 1944 it was clear that the Allies would win. There was another presidential election coming up. Franklin felt he should continue at least until the war was won and the peace arrangements made. He ran again and won.

By April 1945 the war in Germany was practically over, although there would still be hard fighting in the Pacific.

On April 12, Eleanor was at a meeting when the faithful Tommy signaled urgently for her to pick up the phone. The president, who was in Warm Springs, had fainted. Eleanor arranged to fly there immediately, but before she could leave she got a message that Franklin Roosevelt had died.

And yet, as always, her first thought was for others. The vice president was no longer Wallace, but Harry Truman. Eleanor sent a message for Truman to come to the White House immediately. Truman did not know why he had been sent for. She said to him, "Harry, the President is dead."

For a stunned moment Truman could not speak. Then he said, "Is there anything I can do for you?"

She answered with a line that has since become famous. "Is there anything *we* can do for *you*? For you are the one in trouble now."

When Franklin died, Harry S. Truman became president. Eleanor hoped to influence him, as she had often influenced her husband. But Truman was determined to follow an independent course. He did not want to seem to be under Eleanor's influence. Nonetheless, he respected her greatly. Here, they are shown together at Hyde Park.

Chapter 5
LIFE ALONE

ELEANOR ROOSEVELT'S PUBLIC
life did not end when she left the White House.
She had hoped to be able to work with the new
president, Harry Truman, as she had done with
Franklin—making suggestions, giving advice,
introducing him to people whose opinions
might be helpful. But Truman was struggling to
get out from under the shadow of a powerful
and enormously popular president: Franklin D.
Roosevelt. He did not want to appear to be
following Eleanor's lead, so he did not follow up
on the letters she sent him.

*Eleanor Roosevelt in 1957. By now she was greatly admired—a
friend to many rulers and an influential figure in world affairs.*

Nonetheless, he took up many of the New Deal schemes that Franklin and Eleanor had fought for, and today historians believe that Truman was an excellent president.

Even though he did not often take Eleanor's advice, his respect for her was great. In December 1945, only months after Franklin's death, Truman asked Eleanor to serve on the American delegation to the United Nations (U.N.), then only getting started.

Eleanor was not sure that she was equipped for the job, but in the end she took it. She felt, like many people, that the U.N. was the best hope the world had for avoiding another terrible war. Anyway, she would never have been content to "put on my little lace cap and sit by the fire," as she put it. "I think I must have a good deal of my uncle Theodore Roosevelt in me, because I enjoy a good fight."

So she went to work for the U.N. and continued there for six years. She proved she could be tough when she had to be. At one meeting, where Eleanor was chairperson, the Russian delegate kept speaking on and on about how terrible the United States was. "He was an orator of great power," she said, "the words rolled out of his black beard like a river, and stopping him was difficult indeed." But stop him she did.

Eleanor speaking at the United Nations

"I watched him closely until he had to pause for breath. Then I banged the gavel so hard that the other delegates jumped in surprise." She said firmly, "We are here to devise ways of safeguarding human rights. We are not here to attack each other's governments. . . . Meeting adjourned."

She could be tactful, too. Once, for a special United Nations party, a huge cake was brought out, which Eleanor was supposed to cut. Everybody noticed immediately that it was decorated completely with flags of all nations. Which flag would she cut? She cut by the American flag, to everybody's relief.

After she left the U.N., Eleanor found plenty to do. She visited many foreign nations, where she was always treated as if she were a head of state. She worked with many organizations that were working for causes she was interested in. Of course there was her huge family, which included grandchildren and a few great-grandchildren. There was always her mail, her daily newspaper columns, and the large number of friends she had made in her lifetime. She continued to be active in the Democratic party, making speeches at the Democratic conventions in 1956 and 1960.

But age was catching up with her. She began to suffer from a blood ailment, and by 1962 she was in and out of hospitals. Eleanor died that year, at the age of seventy-eight.

The life of Eleanor Roosevelt was not always happy. She had had that grim childhood. Her father, her brother, and an uncle had died of alcoholism.

Eleanor with Prime Minister Nehru of India in 1949

In 1960 Eleanor supported Adlai Stevenson for the presidential nomination over John F. Kennedy, whom she disagreed with on some issues. But Kennedy got the nomination and became president.

In time she and her husband had grown emotionally apart, although they remained close working partners. The marriages of some of her children had not always been happy. She had had more than the usual sorrows that come into people's lives. She once wrote, "There are times, I think, in everyone's life, when the . . . burdens and even the decisions of this life seem overwhelming." But she always managed to rise above her troubles. She believed that to find comfort in life you had to think first of others. She said, "Happiness is not a goal, it is a by-product." It came from working hard for the good of friends, family, community, nation, and even the whole world. And that is what she did.

"I have always seen life personally," she said. She was more interested in people than in ideas. Statistics about poverty or hunger might not awaken her, but the sight of a poor family living in a shack or a thin child going hungry would rouse her to do work beyond the strength of most people. When she saw a wrong, she didn't give up until something was done about it.

At times, of course, she annoyed people, even Franklin, with her demands that this or that person or cause be helped. And there were many Americans of her day who thought that a woman had no business meddling in politics and world affairs. Newspaper cartoons and stories about her were sometimes cruel. But when she died, millions of people in nations around the world felt that they had lost a friend. And indeed they had.

Time Line

1884   October 11: Eleanor Roosevelt is born in New York City.

1894   Eleanor's father, Elliot Roosevelt, dies from alcoholism.

1899   Eleanor enrolls at Allenswood, a boarding school in England.

1905   March 17: Eleanor marries Franklin D. Roosevelt.

1920   Women are granted the right to vote.

1932   Franklin is elected president of the United States.

1945   April 12: Franklin Roosevelt dies. December: Eleanor is asked to serve on the American delegation to the United Nations.

1962   Eleanor Roosevelt dies at the age of seventy-eight.

Author's Note on Sources

Eleanor Roosevelt wrote four autobiographic volumes called, *This Is My Story* (Harper: New York, 1937), *This I Remember* (Harper: New York, 1949), *On My Own* (Harper: New York, 1958), and *Tomorrow Is Now* (Harper: New York, 1963) which can be read by older students. *Eleanor and Franklin*, by her younger friend Joseph P. Lash (Norton: New York, 1971) is formidably long and presents his subject in a very favorable light, but is nonetheless a fascinating study of Eleanor up to the time of Franklin's death. For younger students there is *Eleanor Roosevelt: A Life of Discovery*, by Russell Freedman (Clarion: New York, 1993).

INDEX

About the Author

James Lincoln Collier has written many books, both fiction and nonfiction, for children and adults. His interests span history, biography, and historical fiction. He is an authority on the history of jazz and performs weekly on the trombone in New York City.

My Brother Sam Is Dead was named a Newbery Honor Book and a Jane Addams Honor Book and was a finalist for a National Book Award. *Jump Ship to Freedom* and *War Comes to Willy Freemen* were each named a notable Children's Trade Book in the Field of Social Studies by the National Council for Social Studies and the Children's Book Council. Collier received the Christopher Award for *Decision in Philadelphia: The Constitutional Convention of 1787*. He lives in Pawling, New York.